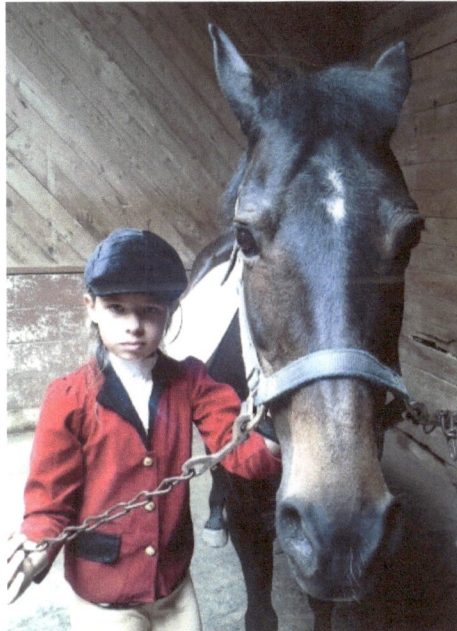

By Margarette Viktoriya Tatur

2016

ABOUT AUTHOR

Hi! My name is Margarette, and I am ten years old. I was born on July 10, 2005. I live in Minnesota, a beautiful state of ten thousand lakes. Even though our lakes spawn millions of mosquitoes every summer, it is still a wonderful place to spend your time, winter or summer. My dad is a very outdoorsy person, and our family enjoys snowmobiling, jet skiing, swimming, camping, boating, and so much more. I also love sports. I take lessons in ballet, gymnastics, and horseback riding. I also love traveling. I have been to several states, but am planning to go overseas sometime to visit Russia and Belarus, where my parents are from.

I live with my mom and dad and two (sometimes very annoying) brothers, Timothy (9) and Aiden (4).

Being homeschooled, we spend much time as a family visiting different places and exploring.

I am an animal lover; I, especially, love horses. One of my biggest dreams is to have two horses and ride them every day. Yes, I am a Horse Crazy Girl, and I enjoy it. Someday, my dream will come true, but until then, I am excited to share my passion with you in this book.

Acknowledgments

I would like to express my gratitude to all who supported me through the process of writing and publishing my first book. Specifically, I want to say thank you to:

My mom, Viktoriya, for her encouragement, help and support, and her contribution as a chief editor and a photographer;

Jacqi Glenn, for professionally editing and proofreading the text;

The Kreuger farm, Dayton, MN, for allowing me to take photos with their gorgeous horses, Devo and Sonatina.

Introduction

As long as I can remember myself, I have been a horse lover. To be more specific, I have been a horse crazy girl (an HCG). I love horses and everything about them. I have collected pictures and magazines with horses, and do not miss an opportunity to pat a horse. I have always thought that this is a very special hobby, as I haven't known too many people who own a horse. The more I grew and met new friends, the more I realized that nearly every other girl is an HCG! The question I started hearing was: What is so special about horses that makes girls attracted to them? I was hearing this question so often that it made me think. This question is exactly what I am set to discover in this special edition: Why Girls Are Crazy About Horses? Whether you are an

HCG or not, I invite you to take this fabulous journey with me. Let's go!

So, what is it about us, girls, dreaming and begging our parents to buy us a horse? Any time I look at a horse, I see gracefulness, strength, power, beauty, character and friendship. I don't know what attracts me more, but I think it's a combination of these characteristics. Could it be that we, girls, and horses share some of these characteristics? If yes, what are they? Keep reading and you will find out.

The question is:

Why Are Girls Crazy about Horses?

Reason #1

Appearance

Horses are Beautiful!!! They are gracious and lovely. Whether a horse is moving or standing, galloping or resting, it's always a stunning view. Speaking of appearance, horses are dressed in a chic and amazingly beautiful variety of colors: white, chestnut, bay, dun, red roan, blue roan, black, mixed colors and markings.

That's attractive to us, girls, isn't it? We just love colors: makeup, shoes, dresses, purses, nail polish, and hair pieces.

But what else makes a horse so outstandingly beautiful? Her legs? Her feet? Her eyes or hooves? To me, it's her mane!!! Horses are ones of a few animals that have a mane. The other animal that is popular for its mane is a lion. What does it tell you? A mane is a symbol of power and wisdom; it is like a crown, making that animal stand out. The mane is the horse's unique gracefulness.

Also, I see a horse's mane as long beautiful hair. Just like mine. And yours. Did you ever see a horse with gorgeous braids with flowers and ribbons? I can't wait to have my own horse so I can fix her "hair."

Reason #2

Personality

When I look at a horse, I always notice how thoughtful and calm she is. It makes me want to talk to her. They are smart and lovable, confident and kind. I just love to be around horses. They are one of the kinds of animals that understand people and cooperate with them. They have a super calming and wholesome effect on a person. For that reason, horses are widely used in rehabilitation centers for emotional and spiritual care.

People start feeling better around horses and get many health benefits. I had a chance to visit one of these centers last summer. There were about eight to ten horses serving people who were in the rehabilitation process from drug addiction. It was interesting; - each horse at this place had overcome some sort of injury and gone through the therapy, and had its own story to share.

Me visiting the Rehab Center. Drawing on a horse symbolizes bringing all our issues and straggles to God. After that the drawing is washed off, which symbolizes how Almighty God takes our struggles and sins away and we are clean again through forgiveness.

Each horse's life was a moving story, and as I listened to them, I couldn't believe how strong horses could be. Strong physically and even stronger spiritually. No wonder they had a profound impact on those needing the same strength to overcome their struggle and fight addiction or physical illnesses. Maybe horses talk in their own way to people or just listen to them, showing support and understanding, but for sure, they know and keep a lot of secrets. I believe that if horses could write, they would keep a diary. Just like girls do!!!

Reason #3

Relationships and social life

Horses are very good at keeping relationships. Did you know that a horse can be your best friend and that you can be hers? They are not only friendly animals; they remember humans for a very long time. In other words, they know their best friends. Isn't that amazing? We, girls, care about friends and love creating new friendships. Horses are the same.

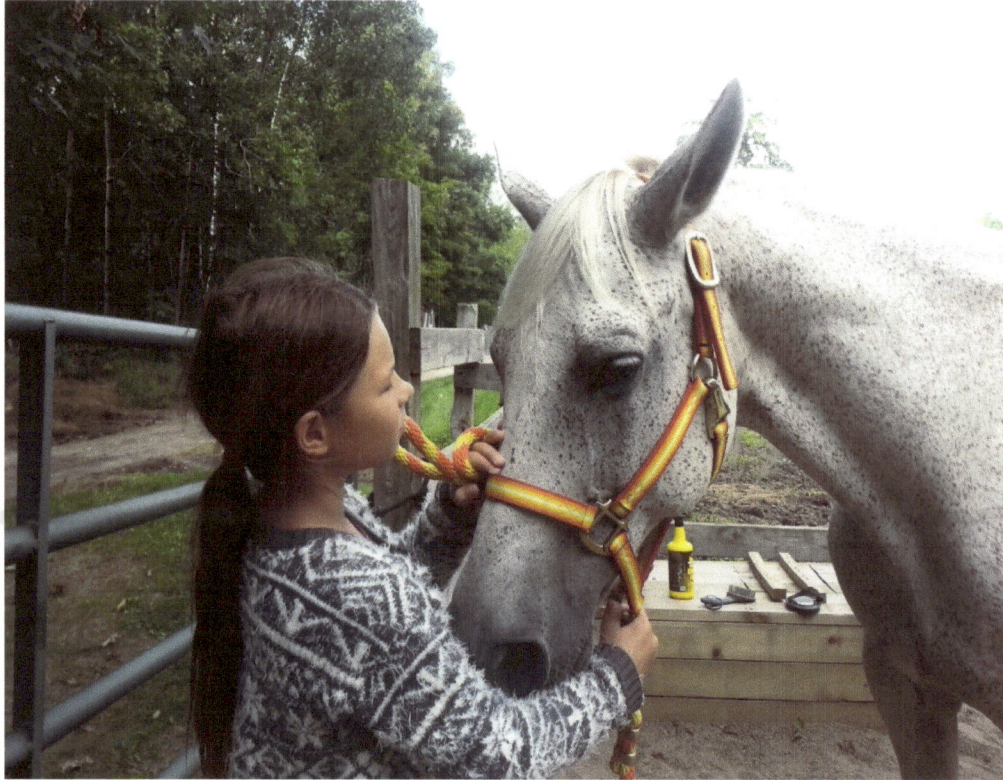

Horses are perfect companions to spend time with, to talk, to take a walk, to ride, or to just hang out.

They are so loveable and loving. Whatever I like doing with my friends, I like doing with the horses: running, laughing, riding, fashion, or taking pictures with them.

Riding a horse is such a pleasure, and yet, it's easy to learn. Horses lift you high and carry you around. That is such an adventure! My most interesting experience with a horse was the very first time I sat on it. It was in Wisconsin Dells, WI. I was riding a horse on the trails through the parks and woods. I felt like a queen, and the horse as my best friend showing me the surroundings of my neighbor state.

Horses are cooperative. They listen to you, they hear you, and do what you ask them to do. They can refuse to listen or to obey someone they don't know. They don't always trust strangers. It happened to me once when I tried to lead a horse which I saw for the very first time. When I approached the horse, grabbing her by the reign, the horse bit me on my arm. It was hurting a little, but it made me feel proud! I took it as a professional accomplishment that left a special mark on my skin. (And if you wonder, yes, I wanted to cry at first, but I didn't). I felt brave and courageous.

Me riding Sonatina, a lovely horse that bit me, summer 2014.

Reason #4

Hardworking

What would people do without horses? Horses are so committed to helping us in so many things. Just think about it: horses spend the most of their lives totally engaged in people's lives, helping to make them better. We see horses entertaining us. We see horses in agriculture. Horses help us to move and to travel. Horses fought in the wars. It all requires an enormous amount of strength and endurance. Horses are so strong that they barely sleep. They are runners. They are swimmers. They are joggers. They are workers. And they are dependable companions.

Girls and women are known to multitask and work hard too: housework and *motherhood, working outside of the house and running millions of errands; sometimes, barely having time for sleep.*

You might think it sounds funny, and I agree, but I can't help, but emphasize that strong connection between horses and femininity.

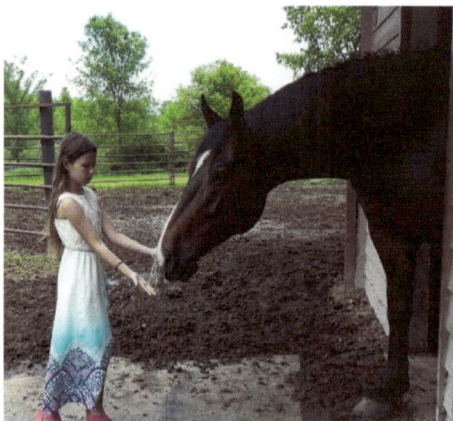

Me feeding Devo, Kreuger Farm, Dayton, MN

These are some reasons I found to explain girls' love for horses. Writing this book was a great adventure for me leading to many new discoveries about horses. I don't know about you, but I have many more reasons to love them even more. As I was writing about horses, I was reading about horses; and as I was reading about horses, I was writing about horses. I even came up with ideas and titles for new books, which might be coming soon.

I hope that you found this book interesting and informative. Feel free to write me back. For now, enjoy my favorite facts about horses.

Random, but my Favorite Facts about Horses:

In the Russian language nouns are divided into 3 groups: feminine, masculine, and neuter? "Horse" belongs to the feminine group;

Sometimes horses can be trained to give a ride without bridals, just people pulling their mane; if you pull the horses' mane, it won't hurt;

Horses are social animals and will get lonely if kept alone;

Horses can sleep both lying down and standing up;

Horses can gallop shortly after birth;

Horses have around 205 bones in their skeleton (human body has 206!)

Horses have bigger eyes than any other mammal that lives on land;

Because horses' eyes are on the side of their head they can see nearly 360 degrees at one time;

Horses gallop at around 44 kph (27 mph);

A male horse is called a stallion; a female horse is called a mare;

A young male horse is called a colt; a young female horse is called a filly.

Source: http://www.sciencekids.co.nz/sciencefacts/animals/horse.html

Some random facts about me; (and please let me know how much we have in common):

- *I speak two languages: English and Russian;*
- *I can ride a four-wheeler, a jet ski, a horse, a bicycle, and my little brother's car;*
- *I am homeschooled;*
- *I don't have a favorite food;*
- *My favorite color is hot pink;*
- *I am a ballerina in the making;*
- *I am a Christian;*
- *I have never broken any bones;*
- *I love catching butterflies in the summer;*
- *I help teach in my mom's preschool class;*
- *I love to read;*
- *I will get a Labrador puppy soon;*
- *I plan my own birthday parties (with my mom's help);*